The Cambridge
Library of Ornamental Art

Arabian Ornament

—The Cambridge—
Library of Ornamental Art

ARABIAN ORNAMENT

from the 12th to the 18th century

Wordsworth Editions

This edition published 1991 by Wordsworth Editions Ltd,
8b East Street, Ware, Hertfordshire.

Copyright © Wordsworth Editions Ltd 1991.

ISBN 1-85326-954-9

Printed and bound in Hong Kong by South China Printing Co.

Acknowledgements

The illustrations in this book are reproduced by kind permission of the Syndics of the Cambridge University Library. They are taken from *L'Art Arabe* by Prisse d'Avennes, and *The Treasury of Ornament* by Heinrich Dolmetsch.

The publishers would like to thank the many staff at the Cambridge University Library who helped in the publication of this book, especially David Hall, Under Librarian (Administration), Nigel Hancock, Head of Reader Services, and Gerry Bye, Head of Photographic Services and his staff.

List of Plates

1. Fourteenth century. Small ornamental carpet.

2. Seventeenth century. Stucco inlays in white marble.

3. Seventeenth century. Mosque of Al-Burdayni: ceiling decoration – interlace patterns.

4. Eighteenth century. Mosque of Amir Shaykhu: wall tiling.

5. Seventeenth century. Dervish tekke: wall tiling.

6. Sixteenth century. Wall tiling: decorative borders.

7. Mihrab from the Mosque of Shaykhu: wall tiling.

8. Twelfth and fourteenth century. Wall mosaics.

9. Thirteenth century. Wall mosaics.

10. Fifteenth century. Mosaic patterns.

11. Fourteenth century. Woven textile.

12. Fourteenth century. Woven textile.

13. Sixteenth century. Ornamentation of a Koran.

14. Eighteenth century. The Bayt (house) of Al-Shalabi. Ceiling decoration.

15. Wooden partitions and borders.

16. Eighteenth century. Fountain of Abd al-Rahman Katkhuda Gamaliyyah: wall tiling.

17. Eighteenth century. Mosque of Sulayman Pasha (Sidi Sariyah): decoration above the door of the minbar.

18. Late eighteenth century. Cut paper work.

19. Sixteenth century. Palace of Ismail Bay: wall tiling.

20. Sixteenth century. Floor mosaics and tiling.

21. Seventeenth century. Painted pottery: studies of flowers and leaves.

22. Seventeenth century. Mosque of Al-Burdayni: freizes and borders from the smaller rooms.

23. Ceiling decoration: arrangement of starred octagons.

24. Seventeenth century. Mosque of Al-Burdayni: ceiling decoration – interlace patterns.

25. Fourteenth century. Mosque of Qawsun: page from a Koran.

26. Eighteenth century. The Bayt (house) of Al-Shalabi: ceiling decoration.

27. Late fifteenth century. Mosque of Sultan of Qayt Bay: ornamentation of doors and cupboards.

Arabian Ornament

IN THE CENTURY after the death of the Prophet Muhammad, his Arab followers spread his teachings through Egypt and North Africa as far west as Spain and as far east as Sassanid Persia. Because of their rapid expansion and the paucity of their own artistic heritage, the Muslims derived their unique style from a synthesis of the arts of the Byzantines, the Copts, the Romans and the Sassanids. The vast interior surface of the Great Mosque of Damascus (714 AD) was covered with stone mosaic in the Byzantine fashion, and the design included such motifs as crowns and fantastic plants and trees. With the movement of the caliph's capital to Baghdad in 750 AD after the rise of the Abassid dynasty the Persian influence became stronger. In the ruins of Samarra lustreware fragments have been found, and the Great Mosque of Al-Qayrawan (c862 AD) is decorated with square lustre tile. The ninth century saw the development of metalwork in Egypt, and from the tenth to the thirteenth centuries the arts of calligraphy, bookbinding, papermaking and illumination were developed there, and Kufic script, animated with interlaced and anthropomorphic designs, became an integral part of artistic expression.

The characteristic that distinguishes Islamic decoration from that of other great civilizations is the predominantly geometric nature of the ornament. The Koranic injunction against the making of images, though questioned by many scholars, has been traditionally interpreted as the forbidding of the depiction of nature, in the belief that the works of God are not to be imitated by man. The nineteenth-century architect and writer Viollet-le-Duc points out that to the invaders of the Byzantine and Roman empires 'These statues, the bas-reliefs, the projected friezes bearing great foliated scrolls intermixed with human and animal figures, must have appeared to the Arabs as monstrous manifestations of the warped imagination of pantheism'. He goes on to say 'Unable to bring to their decorations the world of everyday objects, the image of man, animals or even plants, the artists had but one door open to them – geometry'. This restriction, far from impoverishing the expression of Islamic artists, resulted in the raising of abstract design into an art form not only of enormous wealth and complexity, but of great spiritual purity, and for this purpose geometry in their hands became the creative tool *par excellence*.

Early in the thirteenth century, a school of secular manuscript painting arose near Baghdad with pictures of two types: those that illustrate the scientific works that descended from late Hellenistic models, and those that illustrate anecdotal tales, and whose miniatures represent the true spirit of caricature. After the Mongol invasions there was a revitalization of art through the Chinese taste. The making of artifacts, and textile and carpet weaving, revived throughout Islam, and in Turkey ceramics reached their peak in Izmik ware. The art of Islamic Spain encompassed faience and the intricate lacework of pierced-stone screen windows. The supreme example of this is to be found at the Alhambra Palace at Granada.

The devotion paid by Muslim scribes and artists to the illumination and decoration of the Holy Koran frequently surpasses all but the finest work of their Christian contemporaries. Not only was the text embellished to a remarkably high standard, but the binding of the books was also of the highest quality. Egyptian skill in leathercraft was carried to Europe by way of North Africa, Sicily and Spain, and into the Islamic territories of the Near East. Islamic binding design was at first based on the austerely abstract styles of Coptic leatherwork, employing interlacing bands, knotwork, intricate geometrical arabesques and various Arabic scripts. When artistic leadership of the Islamic world passed to Persia in the later Middle Ages, more colourful decorative styles evolved.

Perhaps the key to understanding the deep satisfaction that comes from the study of Islamic geometrical design is to be found in the observation by Viollet-le-Duc that their cellular patterns resemble those networks of tracery to be found in sections of botanical or animal tissue when examined under a microscope. Unknowingly, the artists of Islam were, perhaps, after all, at a very fundamental level, 'imitating the work of God', and it is our unconscious recognition of this underlying unity which, in design which is at once simple yet immensely complex, gives the art of Islam its timeless beauty and universal appeal.

Arabian Ornament

Plate 1

Plate 2

Plate 3

Plate 4

Plate 5

Plate 6

Plate 7

Plate 8

Plate 9

Plate 10

Plate 11

Plate 12

Plate 13

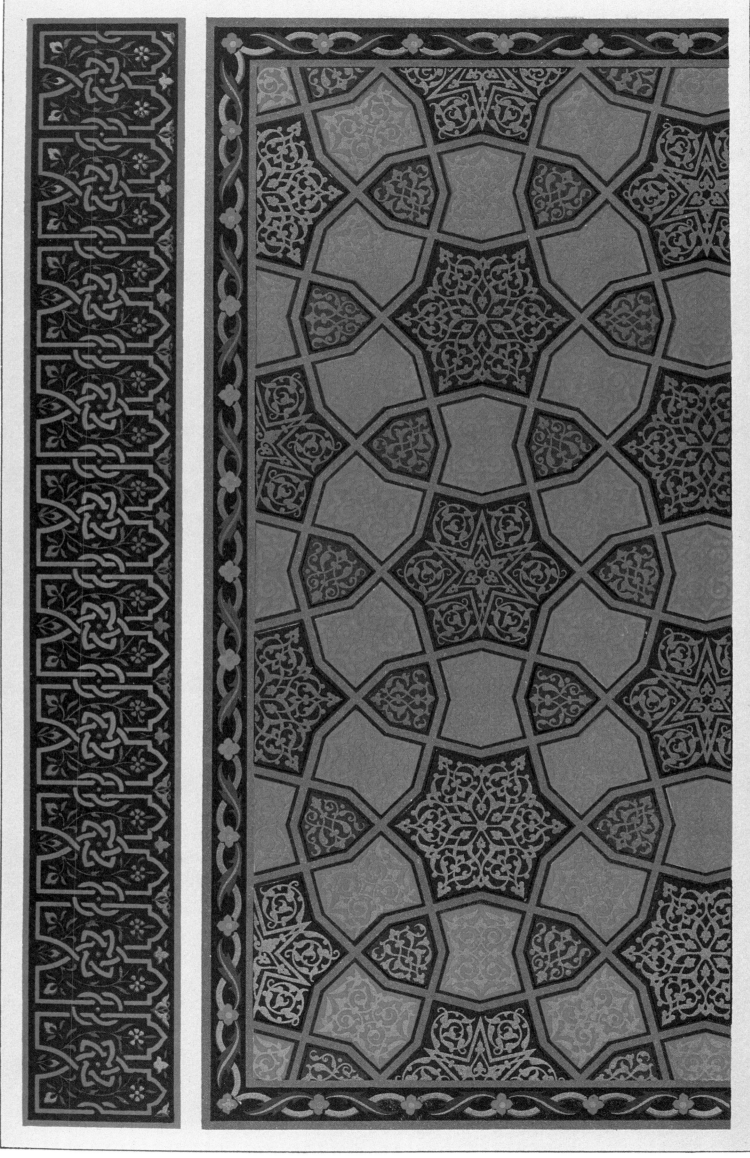

Plate 14

Plate 15

Plate 16

Plate 17

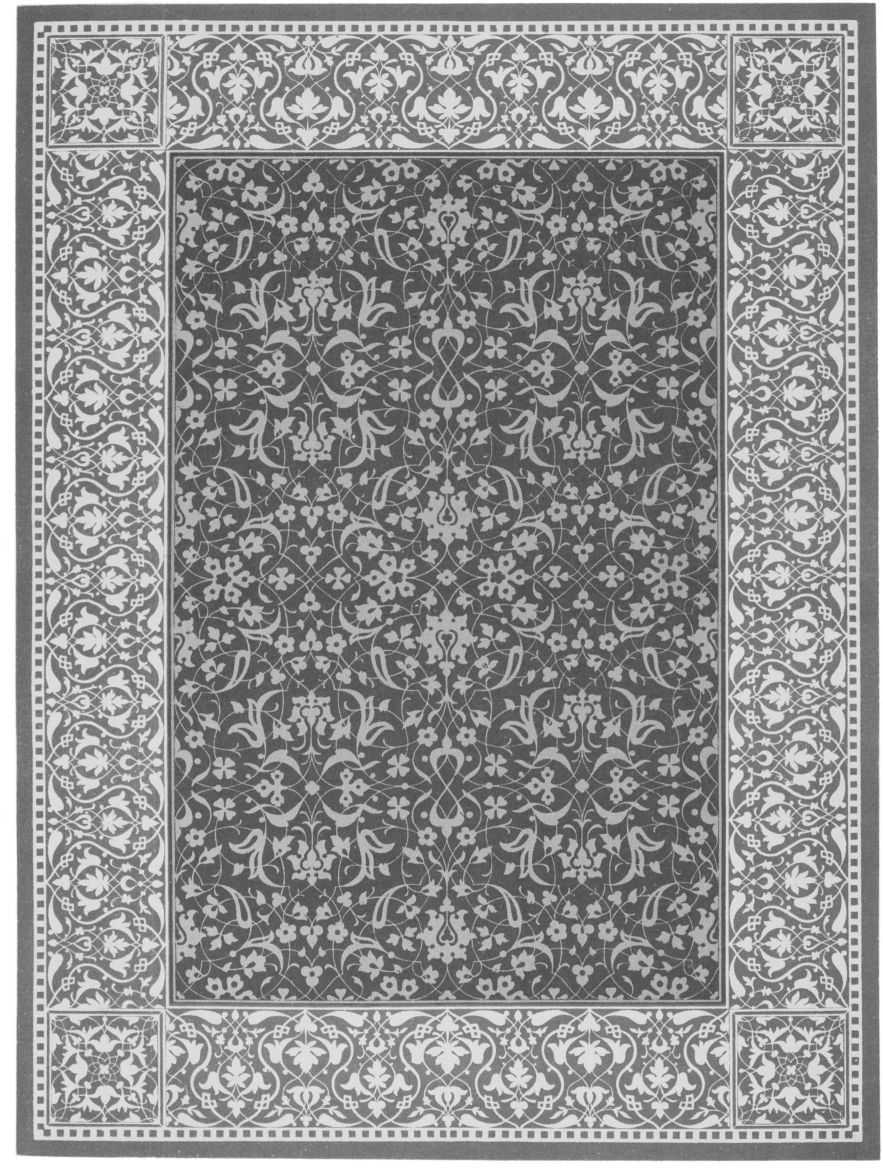

Plate 18

Plate 19

Plate 20

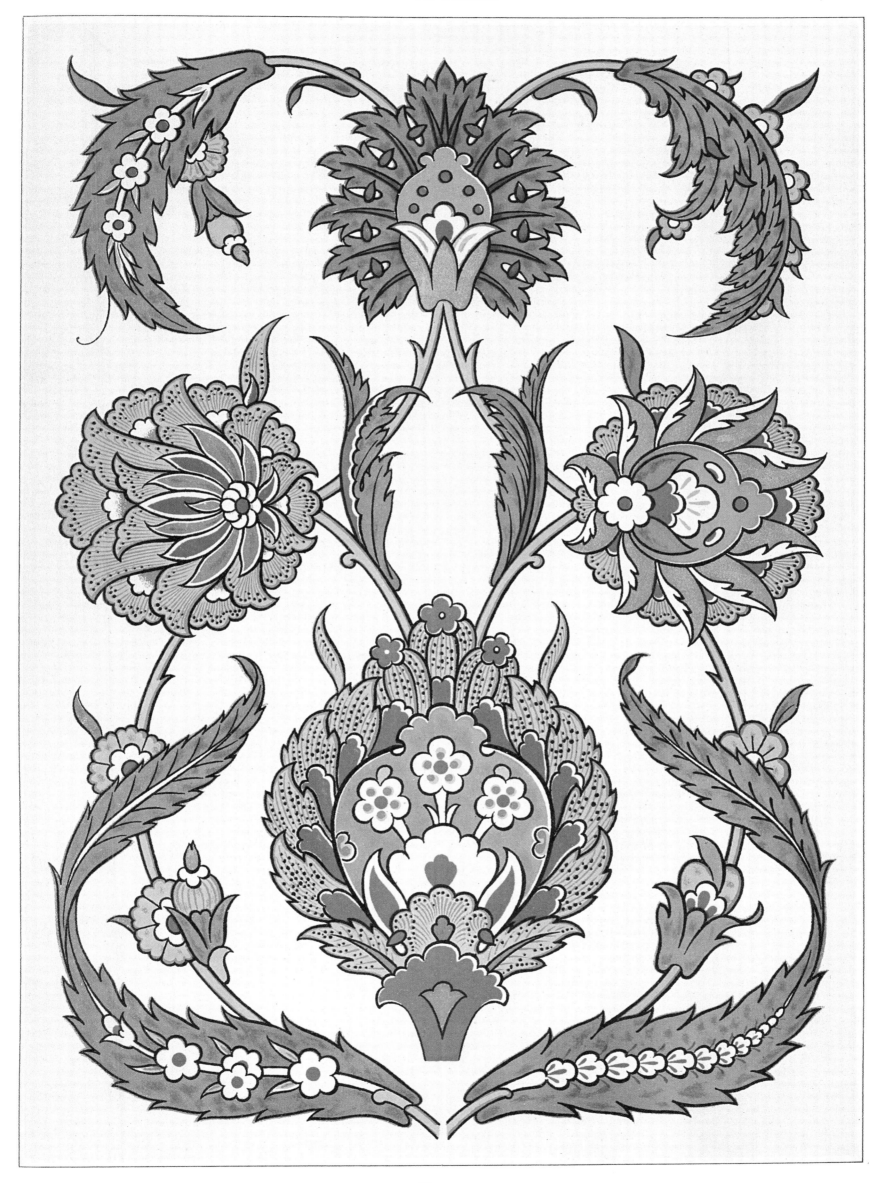

Plate 21

Plate 22

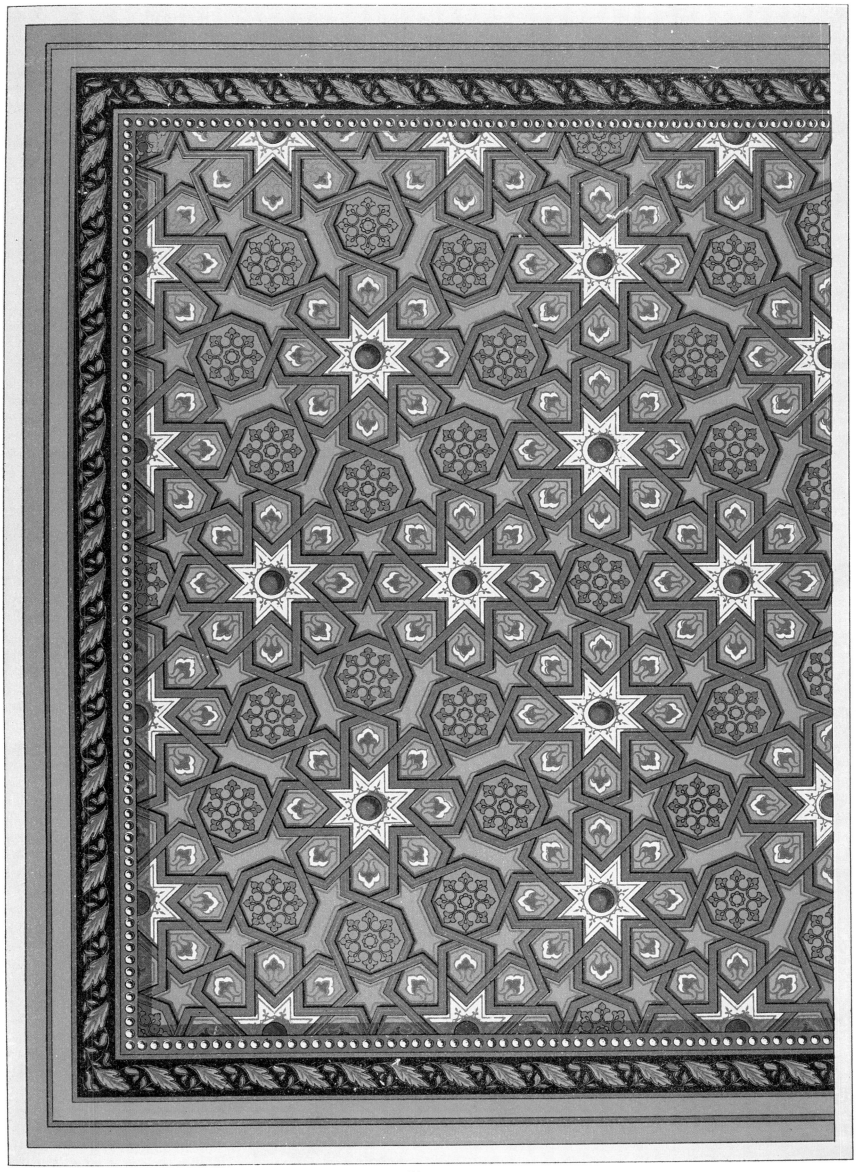

Plate 23

Plate 24

Plate 25

Plate 26

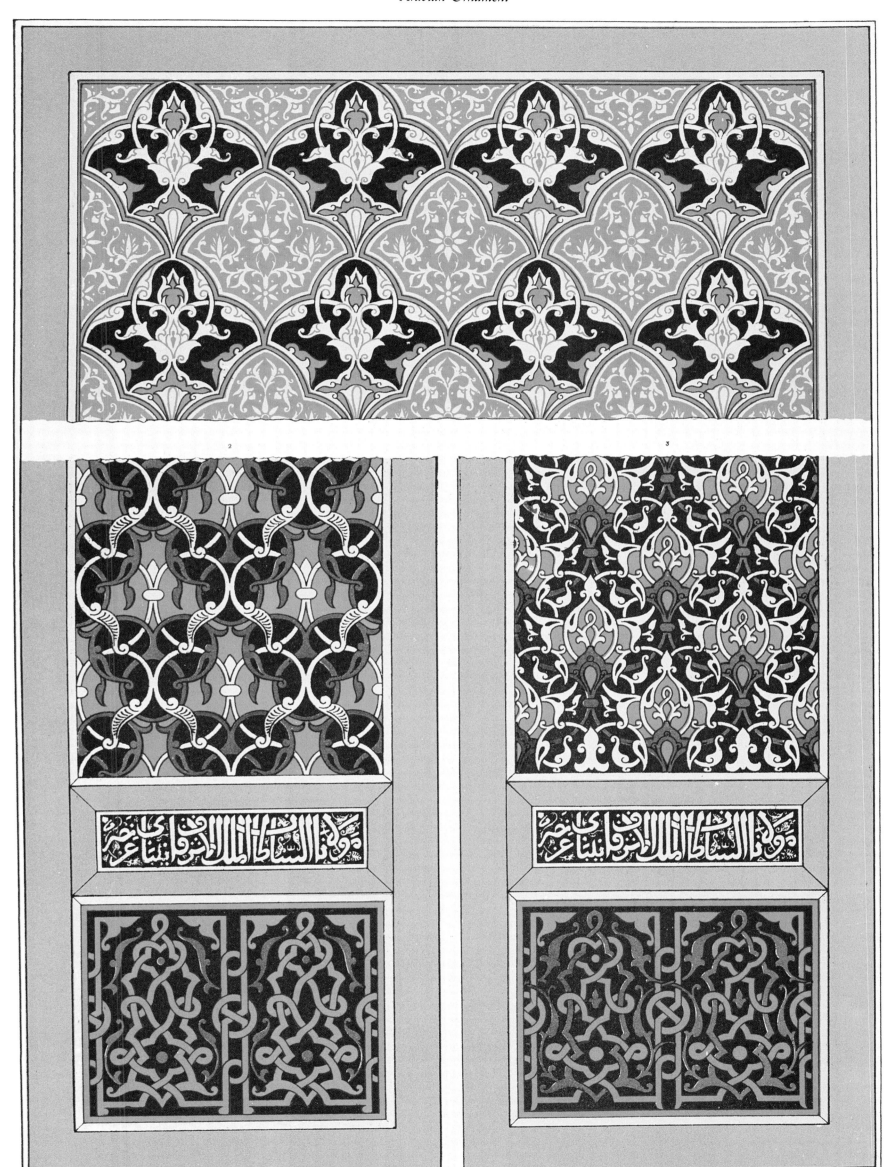

Plate 27

Plate 28

Plate 29

Plate 30

Plate 31

Plate 32

Plate 33

Plate 34

Plate 35

Plate 36

Plate 37

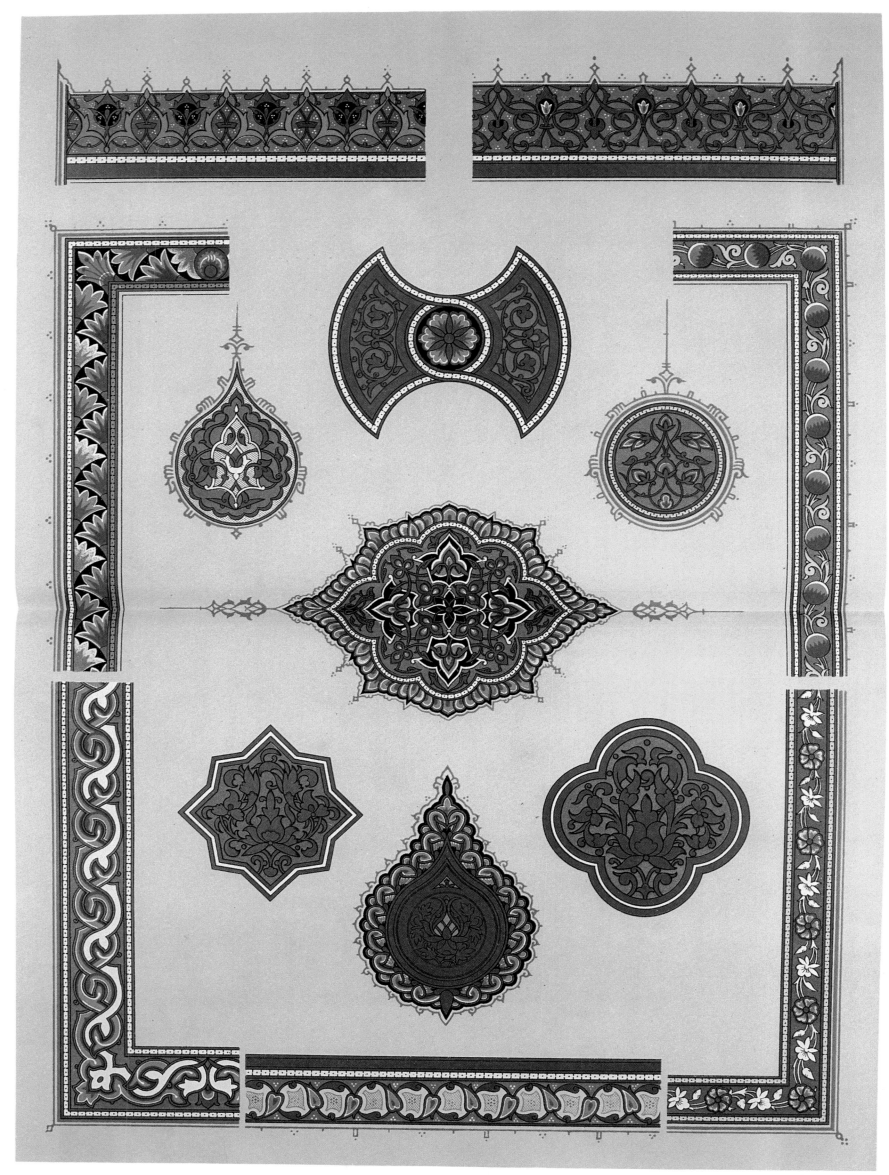

Plate 38

Plate 39

Plate 40

Plate 41

Plate 42

Plate 43

Plate 44

Plate 45

Plate 46

Plate 47

Plate 48